PAMPHLET ARCHITECTURE 32

RESILIENCE

STASUS

JAMES A. CRAIG
MATT OZGA-LAWN

PRINCETON ARCHITECTURAL PRESS
NEW YORK

Published by
Princeton Architectural Press
37 East Seventh Street
New York, New York 10003

For a free catalog of books, call 1.800.722.6657.
Visit our website at www.papress.com.

Printed and bound in Canada by Friesens
15 14 13 12 4 3 2 1 First edition

ART WORKS.
arts.gov

This project is supported in part by an award from the National
Endowment for the Arts.

Editor: Megan Carey
Designer: Stasus

Special thanks to: Bree Anne Apperley, Sara Bader, Nicholas Beatty,
Nicola Bednarek Brower, Janet Behning, Fannie Bushin, Carina Cha,
Russell Fernandez, Linda Lee, Diane Levinson, Jennifer Lippert, Gina
Morrow, John Myers, Katharine Myers, Margaret Rogalski, Dan Simon,
Sara Stemen, Andrew Stepanian, Paul Wagner, Joseph Weston, and
Deb Wood of Princeton Architectural Press —Kevin C. Lippert, publisher

Library of Congress Cataloging-in-Publication Data
Stasus (Firm)
 Pamphlet architecture 32 : resilience / Stasus, James A. Craig, Matt
Ozga-Lawn. — 1st ed.
     p. cm. — (Pamphlet architecture ; 32)
 ISBN 978-1-61689-031-5 (alk. paper)
1. Stasus (Firm) 2. Architectural design—Themes, motives. I. Craig,
James A., 1984– II. Ozga-Lawn, Matt, 1984– III. Title. IV. Title:
Resilience. V. Title: Pamphlet architecture thirty-two.
 NA997.S77A4 2012
 729—dc23
                          2011035715

4   THE RESILIENCE OF RUINS
Mark Dorrian

8   RESILIENCE

14   ARCHITECTURAL FORENSICS

17   Animate Objects

18   Reliquary

22   STILLNESS
Ella Chmielewska

26   ANIMATE LANDSCAPES

26   I: The Site and the Objects

36   II: The Subjects

48   III: Antichronometric Calendar

60   IV: The Room

76   DESIGNING AROUND REMNANTS
Andrew Benjamin

77   Acknowledgments

77   About the Authors

77   Image Credits

The Resilience of Ruins

Mark Dorrian

There is a photograph of a young Polish girl taken in 1948.[1] She stands at a chalkboard, her left arm raised, while she looks over her shoulder toward the camera. Out of the depths of the flat black surface a maelstrom of lines swirl, arriving at last at her hand, which grasps a by-now barely discernable stick of chalk. At the top corner of the chalkboard the name "Tereska" is partly visible. Positioned at the edge of this frame-within-a-frame, it acts to caption both the photograph at which we are looking and the drawing on the board, suggesting that, in the latter, we might be seeing something that is just as much a portrait as—indeed perhaps more a portrait than—the photographic record of the enigmatic face that gazes out at us.

The photographed child is a young refugee who was asked to draw a picture of "home." The image that she makes—if we can call it that—seems a cipher of radical disorientation. What is it that she is doing? Is she in fact drawing some location, or is it perhaps an explosion, or the trails of aircraft overhead? Or might we be more correct if we interpreted her drawing in the most raw and material sense of that word; that is, to see her action as a grinding-down and destruction of the instrument of representation in the face of its inadequacy to the task of showing what has been? Understood in this way, the chalk dust that is smeared on the board and that falls to the ground on which she stands is less a picture than a manifestation of matter that has failed representation and has been failed by it. If dust is the emblem and apparel of all obsolescent and anachronistic things—objects

whose present is past or is still to come—at the same time it itself, as stuff that has been sloughed off, remaindered, and left over, is the epitome of them. In the photograph, the disintegration of the chalk is the assertion—in its purest form—of the materiality of the signifier, which is to say its point of failure and destruction, the point at which representation turns to dust. Chalk may be the stuff with which generations of children have been schooled in the adult world, but here it is the traumatized child who imparts to us a lesson conveyed through this material whose muteness has made it newly eloquent.

Stasus's project, which this pamphlet documents, emerged out of an academic studio that approached Warsaw under the title of the "post-socialist city and its material pre-histories."[2] The photograph of Tereska was presented at the commencement of the studio as a kind of thought-image. In the wake of this, and before traveling to the city for the first time, the studio undertook a project called Architectural Forensics, which invited students to engage in micrological fieldwork in the physical studio space where they would be based and within which their projects would emerge. The materials of the study were the scratches, traces, and dust deposited by previous human and nonhuman occupants of the room, and the project—in its requirement for the close observation of small things—demanded a delicacy of thought and a lightness and agility in the occupation of the space and in the procedures employed in tracking its objects of inquiry. Undertaken in advance of the group's visit to Warsaw, this project aimed to do two things: to bring within the ambit of architectural attention things normally considered to lie beyond its concerns; and to establish the idea that we might consider the physical studio as a kind of "second site" for the emergent projects, one with reference to which they would develop and that they would come to be marked by.

James Craig's and Matt Ozga-Lawn's responses to the project invoked issues of obsolescence, interval, rhythm, and timing that subsequently resonated throughout their work. One response involved a drawing that was made and burned, and the construction of a vessel to hold its remains, while another explored a stop-motion animation of furniture, choreographed in relation to traces on the intensely marked floor of the studio.

Reflection on these themes was elaborated in the following project assignment titled "House for an Inhabitant of Warsaw," which was intended to give students a foothold in the various locations in the city in which they had begun to work. Here, Craig and Ozga-Lawn counterposed an appropriated metronome—which served as a house for a timekeeper and set in motion the rhythms that would come to pattern the entire project—with a house for a guide. Importantly, these were situated within—and in the case of the guide's house, made from materials excised from—a wooden chest, the first of a series of furniture elements that began to accumulate within the project, mediating between Wola, the area of Warsaw to which the project was

addressed, and the "second site" of the studio. From this point on, everything that was made came to operate simultaneously at two scales: the 1:1 of the furniture elements and the studio, and the conventional architectural scales (1:500, etc.) at which the site was graphically constituted.

Looking over the work, in retrospect it seems to me that the choice of site by Craig and Ozga-Lawn was motivated at a certain level by a refusal of representation, or at least by a refusal to draw over the area with the sort of urbanism that they saw already encroaching on its edges. Far from providing a reassuring picture in accord with official narratives of Poland's post-1989 westward-looking aspirational entrepreneurialism, they sought instead an approach that could hold back the impending development of the site. In the face of this, they insisted on the importance and necessity of the gap that the place established within the city and the interval for thought that it offered. As their project developed, it drew upon the strange imagined half-lives of discarded things in order to develop a proposition for this large disused industrial zone in inner-city Warsaw, within which a complex of decaying infrastructural installations traced sequences of fraying spatial figures. In it they found a world of flickering, palpitation, and silences that gathered before being discharged in sudden convulsions. Here, stillness accumulated in the city in the same way as the intervals between the tick of a clock in an empty room gradually and unbearably intensify before their release. In this place, things— footsteps, breath, the thud of the heart—took on a strange new clarity because the spacing between them had assumed a new consequence.

This special quality of rhythm came to underlie Stasus's proposal for an urban-scale studio and filmic landscape, whose scope runs from the momentary passage of a train—the anorganic shuddering of which vivifies the animation building—to the slowly gathering momentum of the film festival, whose cosmic-mythic sweep circumscribes the multiplicity of events that rhythmically pattern the site. As this advances, elements within the landscape of objects that Stasus inserts within the site come in turn to life and begin to oscillate and hum with varying harmonics before falling once more out of use and into silence.

This project is a dream of things in which the viewer plays the role of the dreamer. Uncertain of whether we are at the scale of the city or the scale of a room, we are—in part because of this—taken to the heart of things that lie close to hand: precisely the kind of fragile, intimate objects (a chair, a table, a toy box) that disappeared with the systematic erasure of domestic space in Warsaw's midcentury trauma. It is the virtue of Stasus's proposition that it makes and holds a clearing in the contemporary city that allows the resounding of something simultaneously opaque and of startling clarity, whose instruments are these obsolescent and anachronistic things that are charged with the future and imbued with the resilience of ruins.

Mark Dorrian is Professor of Architecture Research at Newcastle University.

1. The photograph was taken by Chim (David Seymour), as part of a project commissioned by UNICEF. Tereska was a resident at an institution for disturbed children in Otwock, which lies to the southeast of Warsaw. I discuss this image in the introduction to Mark Dorrian and Ella Chmielewska, eds., "Warsaw: Tracking the City," *The Journal of Architecture* 15, no. 1 (February 2010). **2.** The studio ran at the University of Edinburgh between 2007 and 2009. There is an overview of the work in Mark Dorrian, *Warszawa: Projects for the Post-Socialist City* (Edinburgh: Cityspeculations, 2009).

Resilience

Site plan overlaid onto Luftwaffe photograph of Warsaw taken in 1944

Site plan overlaid onto aerial photograph taken in 2008

A surface reading of the term "resilience" suggests a certain kind of immunity to trauma, a shrugging-off of the chaos of events—a bouncing back. It is a term that largely escapes rigorous inquiry and is more often used as a label establishing the positive properties of something. On closer examination, the meaning of the word (and that which it is applied to) becomes less clear. Is a resilient individual one who adjusts quickly to new circumstances or one who suppresses all memory of trauma? Is a resilient material fundamentally altered during the event but, like elastic, not after—and what of a resilient city?

The positivity of the term is necessarily challenged by this inquiry, and a less certain meaning of "resilience" emerges. For although something must appear unchanged in order to convey the trait, the resilient thing is in fact always irreversibly altered. Our interest in resilience is that this alteration and process of transformation need not be a visible material change, but can also be brought about by a shift in ideological circumstance, a representational choice, a metaphysical linkage. While the trauma may not change the object as such, knowledge of the trauma is often enough to alter it. It is the very possibility of an object to embody multiple stages and conditions of interpretation that makes it exciting as a design tool. Rather than simply looking at physical resilience, then, the inquiry also is directed at how alterable an object is while maintaining the qualities that define it. It is in these qualities that we may find resilience.

A bullet-strewn wall surface in Warsaw photographed in 2007

Stasus is interested not just in the material conditions of things but in the additional layers of meaning that collect around and between them. Approaching an apparently vacant site in a city as complex and historically layered as Warsaw becomes further complicated by the nature of these found resiliencies. It could be said that an apparently vacant site has a metaphysical occupancy through the various fragments and material traces that are scattered and embedded throughout; a layer of dust on a windowsill, a bullet hole in a stone wall, or the profound additional meanings attached to disused rail tracks in the city. It is by studying these attributes that we can build and accumulate an archive of possibilities with which to develop design proposals that register the properties of the site while contributing to the creation of something new.

Stasus views design as a process of navigating the resistances produced by such possibilities. We are insistently reluctant to force simple concepts onto projects and their sites. We aim to identify and work with that which in some form already exists. Our process is initially one of identification—revealing the resilient traces and resulting resistances within the scope of our intended investigation. We test and explore the properties found in these existing conditions. The more resistant certain elements are to transformation, deletion, or manipulation, the more they are worked into the design process and become integral to design outputs. These outputs don't necessarily signify a finality; in fact, it is their lack of influence as a destination

The animation of props and screws by the Brothers Quay reveals the secret lives of objects

We consistently acknowledge our influences in this process—architectural, filmic, literary, anecdotal. To do otherwise would be to conceal our role as designers. A major part of establishing the connections between the elements we are working with is in the recognition of where they intersect with the references we accumulate in our thinking. The positioning of that which we are interested in and influenced by in relation to our own material often challenges our work more directly, while also allowing for a reinterpretation of the source material itself. In this way, our influences are treated as design tools in the same manner as found objects, to be delineated and integrated within our process. Their most resilient qualities will enable design.

The Brothers Quay, as animation filmmakers, often appear to animate through the inherent material characteristics of the objects that they have chosen to engage, rather than focusing simply on symbolism or connotations. The interference and manipulation of these objects dictate the manner in which the brothers start to move through animation, and the filming and animating of the elements act as a mode of revealing the apparent nature of the objects they are working with. Storyboards, scripts, and other planning devices are rarely, if ever, used. We aspire to do the same with our processes—alter, record, study, and alter again. The intention, and result, is often necessarily unclear. Over the course of the two-year studio-based study described here, many references and influences were tested on the project and vice versa—a challenge to the resiliency of the ideas

that enables a certain kind of freedom within the process itself.

The approach is significantly different from a "blank paper" (*tabula rasa*) methodology. Rather than creating our own clearing for design work, we aim to identify the most resilient elements within our field of exploration. These may be meanings passed through material context, implied mythical narratives, incidental connotations, and historical and prehistorical implications.[1] As such, our design landscape is not only a physical landscape, but an immaterial one, both visceral and cerebral. Our design process therefore could be described as an investigation of the resilient qualities drawn out from that which already exists.

embedded within these references as well as within our own work.

The studio, as a second site that mediates between the site of the project and the desires of the architectural thinker, gains a special significance in this mode of inquiry. If the chosen site is no longer seen as a "blank page," then increased attention must also be turned to the specificities of the studio context and the representational media utilized within. It is appropriate then that the principal project of this book is preceded by two smaller projects tasked with examining the studio through the metaphor of forensics. Mark Dorrian introduced the concept of architectural forensics in the studio brief that instigated these initial projects. In focusing our attention on the smallest detail in these examinations of the studio, Dorrian shifted our architectural training onto that which we would typically disregard—everything (tape, paint spills, dust) now had a potential. The intrinsic attention devoted to the space and our resulting projects, Animate Objects and Reliquary, were important in providing us with a particular set of investigative equipment to take with us to Warsaw.

Warsaw can be seen as embodying the complexities surrounding the given condition of resilience. It would be an error to respond to the city through a simple misreading or surface reading of what the city's contemporary condition represents, or to define this condition as "resilient" in the common usage of the term. We were fortunate not to begin our study through the distancing of a particular analysis,

Katy Bentall's studio at 36 Smolna Street, Warsaw

but rather from within an interior space at 36 Smolna Street—from within an artist's studio built into, and remaining in, a ruined building. In this space, housing both the work of a contemporary artist and the work and archives of the previous occupant, a socialist realist sculptor, we found intricate layers of material complexities. Fresh from our forensic study of the studio in Edinburgh, our senses were finely tuned to details of the space, particularly the resilient quality of the materials that constituted it. In this studio, artwork and architecture merge as extensions of each other, their combined histories overlapping or being pressured in juxtaposition. Built into the ruin of a bombed building, the studio survives in a vulnerable, precarious state. It is where the contemporary meets not only one past but many. These prehistories are evident throughout, constituting an indivisible whole, down to the tiles that make up the floor (relocated postwar from a demolished building on Marszałkowska Street). This first view of Warsaw, in and through the lens of this space, both physical remnant and allegory for the city and its material prehistories, provided a focused perspective on the city as we sought a site for further investigation.

We found our site on a cold, gray morning during an unplanned excursion to the west of the city that took us to the subdistrict of Czyste in Wola. We had walked out of the busy city center, crossing disused railway tracks and abandoned lots and entering a deserted, desolate landscape tinted in rust by the many industries that had once occupied it. We wandered between and around railway carriages, small memorials, and two nineteenth-century redbrick gasometers. Czyste, translated as "clear," gave us our clearing in the city, a vast emptiness that appeared counter to the Warsaw we were exploring. It seemed to contain, confront, and embody the city in some indefinable way, and it affected us as profoundly as the studio on Smolna Street. Beyond the ash-black trees on the site boundary stood the towers of the expanding and encroaching financial district, a forceful reminder that the landscape was under threat from a new occupation—and that time was ticking.

Our project, Animate Landscapes, is the main focus of this pamphlet. It is our response to this landscape and its seemingly unique condition in the city. Our proposal emerged through a long and complex process of investigation, first born through a determination to protect and preserve the site and then through the possibilities of its reuse and reinterpretation. The development of the project over time began to animate the landscape in different ways; the pace of the project's progress became directly linked to the proposal itself. Ultimately, we proposed that the site would become the location of an institute of experimental film, a program inspired firstly by the rich history of animation and experimental filmmaking in Poland and Eastern Europe and secondly by the processes we used in the studio itself—photography, stop-motion animation, projection—which became the integral means of how the project came into being. This approach developed into a formative methodology that looked to the potential of the object, the studio, and the design process as tools to produce a new, resilient architecture.

---

1. Mark Dorrian framed "prehistory" as an operative term in relation to the studio investigation of Warsaw, referring to the multiple layers of material history present in the complex (postsocialist) city.

Architectural Forensics

The Studio as Site

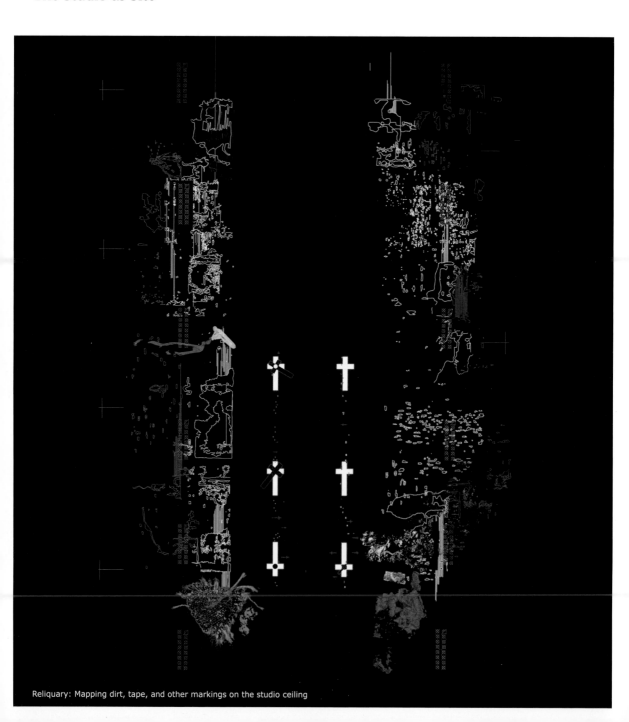

Reliquary: Mapping dirt, tape, and other markings on the studio ceiling

Alphonse Bertillon, exhibition at the 1983 World's Columbian Exposition. This image was presented to us as an epigraph to the Architectural Forensics project.

The studio is a key site of architectural production, yet it is not often thematized or reflected upon in any rigorous way. Typically it is considered to be a kind of neutral space, and certainly it is rarely considered to have any consequence or effect upon the work that is produced in it. Architectural projects, addressed to and destined for sites that are "out there" in the world beyond the studio, seem to by-pass or efface it and the conditions of their own production. Perhaps in some ways this is a symptomatic response to a threat that is part and parcel of a constructive practice that works through representation. Architectural projects are conceived and developed for specific locations through drawings, models, etc. But they are always apart from the sites for which they are destined and hence are necessarily dislocated from them. They emerge in the alterior place of the studio and have to be transmitted (via discursive and graphic techniques, etc.) to the sites upon which they will ultimately be built. The studio thus appears as a kind of space of transmission, a space through which something has to be sent, which would suggest that to admit it into the architectural project, and to welcome its effects, would be something akin to welcoming interference on a telephone line.

—Mark Dorrian, programmatic brief, 2007

We responded to the challenge of forensic investigation individually, finding our respective sites in the two liminal planes of the studio space: the floor and the ceiling. Together, these planes framed the studio, suggesting possibilities of relationships and reflections between the markings, the inscriptive approaches, and our methodologies.

Stills from stop-motion animation

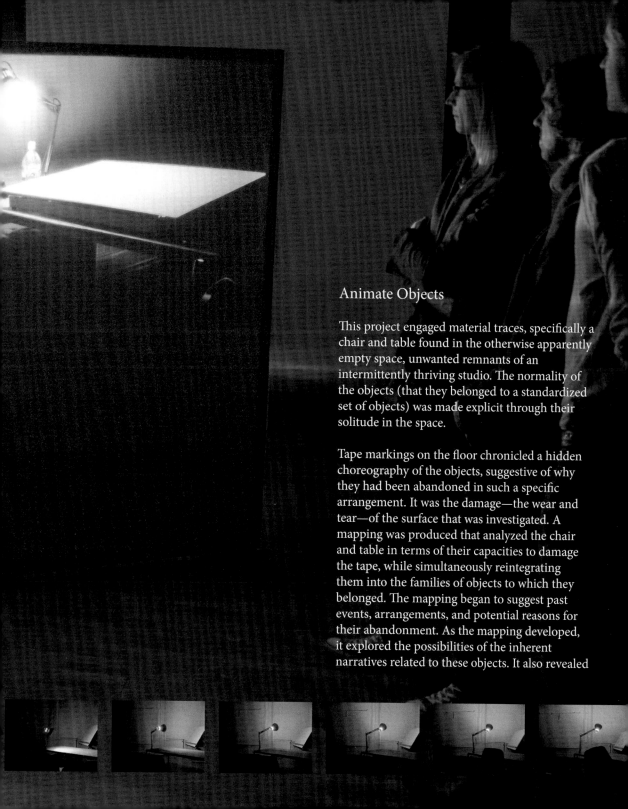

Animate Objects

This project engaged material traces, specifically a chair and table found in the otherwise apparently empty space, unwanted remnants of an intermittently thriving studio. The normality of the objects (that they belonged to a standardized set of objects) was made explicit through their solitude in the space.

Tape markings on the floor chronicled a hidden choreography of the objects, suggestive of why they had been abandoned in such a specific arrangement. It was the damage—the wear and tear—of the surface that was investigated. A mapping was produced that analyzed the chair and table in terms of their capacities to damage the tape, while simultaneously reintegrating them into the families of objects to which they belonged. The mapping began to suggest past events, arrangements, and potential reasons for their abandonment. As the mapping developed, it explored the possibilities of the inherent narratives related to these objects. It also revealed

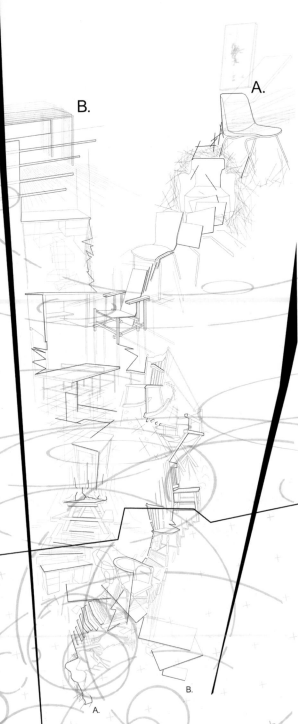

B.

A.

B.

A.

Choreographic mapping

how these narratives, through exaggeration and manipulation, could become dominant over the material traces left behind, and start to act as a controlling force or script for movements. This scripted history was re-created in a stop-motion animation in which actors were replaced by narrative-infused things.

Through this observation, the meanings inferred from the familiar objects were questioned, creating the potential for these meanings to become more resilient than the objects themselves. The rules and implications of the elements continued to feed a process even after they were no longer physically present—the transmission from material to meaning (and back again).

Reliquary

The reliquary protected a residual trace of previous activity in the studio—a small piece of cloth. A mapping of the material traces left by years of work within the studio generated a particular kind of attention to the detailed landscape of its interior surfaces. The traces analyzed were those related to the suspension of years of project work: vestiges of tape, pins, hooks, and rope. As an inverted terrain, skylights (and the scum pools upon them) were incorporated into this mapping. During this process, the cloth stood out as a vibrant remnant of something no longer present. On closer inspection, the material appeared as a fibrous organ, akin to a beating heart. Through a mapping of the piece in-situ, a reversal of implied importance within the studio was created. This cloth played a pivotal role, ultimately forming a memorial to the work that had been undertaken in the space, a miniature but resilient trace of what had come before.

Like the ancient reliquaries, which often contained pieces of clothing from saints, a casket was constructed to demonstrate, in exaggerated form, the protection of this artifact. The casket

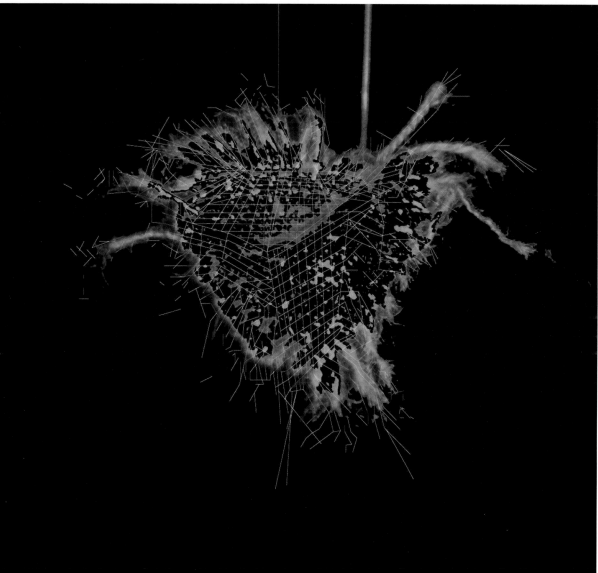

The cloth enhanced

The cloth in-situ

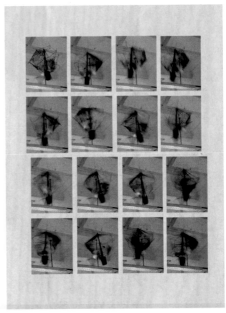

The reliquary, suspended with mapping and stylus
Opposite: Detail of the reliquary

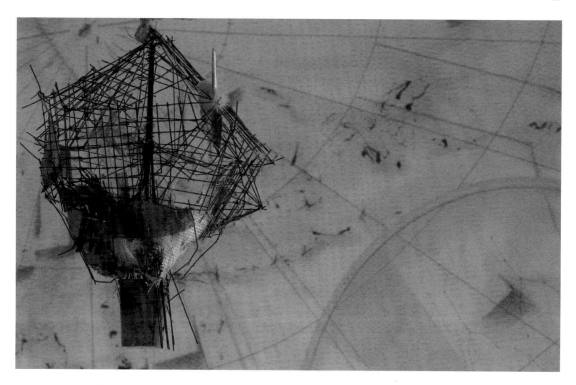

took the form of a scaled-up version of the element within, a structure that manipulated the implications of the originating object via its transmittal through scale. The reliquary was suspended with a counterweighted stylus that burned the mapping of the ceiling traces. The mapping was destroyed by the operation of the stylus—the drawing tool turning representation to ash. The reliquary captured this ash of inscription and embedded it with a renewed meaning that surpassed the original representation. Through its preservation and simultaneous removal and dematerialization, the context of the studio was equalized and skewed so that a discarded element, in this case a small piece of cloth, took on a heightened, sacred significance. The simultaneous mapping and preservation of the cloth through this reliquary acted as a metaphor for the resilient nature of the studio as a site—a place where design potential was embodied in absolutely everything and so nothing should be discounted.

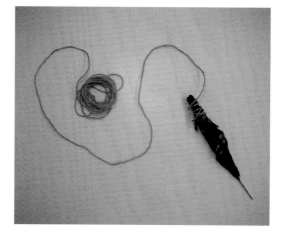

Our close examination of objects, material traces, representational qualities, metaphysical properties, and potentialities found within the familiar space of the studio generated a methodological toolkit that we could take to Warsaw and enabled a new way of viewing and exploring the city.

Stillness

Ella Chmielewska

"Matter never makes jokes: it is always full of the tragically serious....But the resemblance, the pretense, the name reassures us and stops from asking...."[1] For Bruno Schulz, whose haunting stories, like afterimages, persist etched in the memory of his readers, the matter already carries its concerns, its own stories and accounts; in its depths, "tensions build up, attempts at form appear."[2] Schulz's writing—infused with architectonic sensibility and material imaginary—summons places and objects that are vulnerable, porous, furnished with memory, open to emotional stirrings. His streets are shadowed by anxieties, houses shudder with premonitions, the floor counts its parquet tiles, and chairs frown and wink meaningfully. His surfaces are weary, "bored with the incessant changes in all the cadenzas of rhythm...susceptible to distant, dangerous dreams"; they witness the chatter of domestic objects, anticipate reticent meetings of things, command new tales where "[t]he essence of furniture is unstable...and receptive to abnormal temptations."[3]

Stasus's attention to materialities and the dynamic properties of found objects and inscriptive surfaces persisted since the Architectural Forensics project, from where ideas emerged that were carried over to Warsaw. For Ozga-Lawn, objects of furniture, in their imagined nocturnal movements, both animated and accounted for traces on the floor in the Edinburgh studio, and through those traces, spatial and material memories were apprehended in time-based investigations. In Craig's Reliquary, material reflection on modalities of representation, in-scribing and de-scribing, and the physical states of drawing out and drawing in, of collecting and holding the documentary remains, remained paramount. Together, choreographic objects, cartographic surfaces, and scenographic imageries were considered through the measure of movement and repose, rhythms of stillness and containment, calibrations of attention to material remembering, imagining, and comprehending. These explorations anticipated Warsaw's fragile materialities first encountered in an artist's studio on Smolna Street.[4] There, the city's postwar memories and (pre)histories could be seen in particularly sharp relief. They surfaced in adjacencies, in proximities and colocations with personal stories and encounters materialized in art making, writing, and positioning of texts and things.

The site selected for the project in Wola was a found site, a place that was stumbled upon, that resisted instant apprehension and raised as yet unarticulated questions. In its felt qualities, the site suggested properties of persisting that developed in the way Stasus came to conceptualize resilience: finding and holding of a clearing, simultaneously an opening in understanding, an aperture in ways of considering the properties of the site, and a potentiality for beholding. This site was not a mere physical gap in urban landscape, but a material condition of *gapness*, where the impending damage to the surface was as critical to consider as the capacity inherent in the site's endurance, in survival *in damage*. For Stasus, resilience is about the significance of things, holding on to properties that matter on and for the site; it is about *mattering* of things, about things standing in the way, materially objecting the loss of meaning, persistent in their resisting.

When one encounters it, the project's site in Wola is striking in its weighty stillness. The force of the city pressing upon it is palpable. But there is another source of the eerie calm there; the site is a border-zone of trauma. In its stillness, the desolate landscape gapes in incomprehension. It had seen the unimaginable and had frozen in horror. The Wola massacre, perpetrated in August of 1944 by SS-Sturmbrigade Dirlewanger, has been measured in the weight of human ashes.[5] The memory of the events endures through material absence: looted and burned down tenements, missing walls and courtyards that witnessed the killings. No representation is adequate. Only found objects are able to speak, potentially animating memories of the site, affording possibilities of thinking and of making. On the edge of the trauma, between the absent tenements and the remaining train tracks that directed the forced movement of people and things out of the city toward death or displacement, is the site of still felt absence, persisting disquiet. It is a site of in-between, a gap between the inquiry and the impossibility of representation, between landscape and objects, fragility and endurance. This condition of indeterminacy, of in-between, speaks to the vulnerability of Warsaw's surfaces and its sites, the constant of the material loss, the chronic premonition of forced displacement, continuing threat of erasure and relocation.

Philosopher Michel Serres pins down the location of "self" in the embodied realization of being in between.[6] The sensible thinking is contingent on his position in relation to objects present around him: "Knowing things requires one first of all to place oneself between them… in the midst of their mixture, on the paths that unite them."[7] This knowing demands an intimate, close contact with the surfaces of things, surface on surface, a kind of positional thinking that is situated in between. For Serres, material surface is alert, perceptive in its contingency; it is "the place where exchanges are made, the body traces the knotted, bound, folded, complex path, between the things to be known."[8] The contingent inquiry in the midst of which Stasus is situated is a mixture, where things, traces, surfaces, and thoughts mingle with one another. It is a coming together, unfolding: a condition of meeting in "common contingency" that reveals positions, proximities, adjacencies of types and forms of inquiring mingled bodies and objects.[9] In this revealing, thinking (and making) surfaces.

Inside the studio on Smolna Street, a plaster cast, a giant mask of a child's face, rests on the seat of a bentwood chair. Poised on the patterned stone floor, with other objects of the studio in the background, the chair is part of an ephemeral grouping in a composed interior. The space of the photograph registers quietude, stillness, a sense of composure. Nothing in the frame, in this interior, or among these objects suggests anxiety, distress, or trauma. Events, tensions, and intentions are disclosed within the larger frame, in adjacencies, contingencies, and movements. The floor tiles are unlikely migrants, but they are survivors of past expropriations and demolitions, relocated, like furnishings (*meble*), from the previous studio demolished to make way for the communist parade grounds. The stone floor remembers its prewar location, and Warsaw's first postwar gallery, Salon Nike, visited by Picasso in 1948. Moved from an intact building that survived in the wrong place, the floor had been saved by relocating into a ruin on the site of (still) impending development. The chair's history is unknown. An ordinary, portable object, it could have come from a bistro cafe nearby. It could have been found in the ruins, in Warsaw's wartime "wonderland of destruction," among scattered fragments of private lives: "women's clothes, picture frames, chairs, medicine bottles, a hairbrush, all blown out of windows and knocked away from near brick or stone on contact with the ground."[10] The cast gazes upward where the skylight indexes the missing floors above. Created in the studio for the sculpture on Marszałkowska Street, it is the least traveled object from the group. Its itineraries are local, though in its continuous repositioning within the studio, it is relentlessly referencing both the city outside and the archives contained in this fractured building.

Indexing the city's public and private histories and geographies, touching the surfaces that matter, the objects gathered in the studio, like those developed for the site in Wola, persist in their material knowing—each charged with memory that endures, that stills, each insisting on making things matter. The stillness in the studio, and in the methodology proposed by Stasus, is not about silence or absence of motion, but about the condition of resilience, of persistence in (fragile) materiality, in making, and in the still-ness of things.

Ella Chmielewska teaches cultural and visual studies at the University of Edinburgh School of Architecture.

1. Bruno Schulz, *The Street of Crocodiles*, trans. Celina Wieniewska (New York: Walker and Company, 1963), 64–65. Schulz was a Polish writer and artist, killed in his hometown of Drohobycz by a Gestapo officer in 1942. His writing has influenced the work of numerous visual artists, including the Brothers Quay. **2.** Ibid., 59. **3.** Ibid., 67. **4.** Katy Bentall's studio is the first space explored in Warsaw. Created in the atelier built by her late father-in-law, sculptor Karol Tchorek, within a ruin, the space is simultaneously Bentall's studio, a listed place of cultural heritage, and an archive. See Ella Chmielewska et al, "A Warsaw Address: A Dossier on Smolna Street," *The Journal of Architecture* 15, no. 1 (February 2010), 7–9. **5.** Karol Tchorek's documentation of the commemorative sites of wartime executions in Warsaw, Tchorek-Bentall Foundation. On Tchorek's commemorative tablets see Ella Chmielewska and Sebastian Schmidt-Tomczak, "The Critical Where of the Field," in *Architecture and Field/Work*, ed. Suzanne Ewing et al (London: Routledge, 2010), 101–9. **6.** Michel Serres, *The Five Senses: A Philosophy of Mingled Bodies*, trans. Margaret Sankey and Peter Cowley (London: Continuum, 2008), 19, 23. **7.** Ibid., 80. **8.** Ibid. **9.** Ibid. **10.** The landscape of ruins and the Wola massacre described in Ian MacMillan, "Warsaw, Poland. Early October, 1944—The City of Stories," *Chicago Review* 37, no. 2/3 (1991), 78. In *The Captive Mind*, Czesław Miłosz also recalls the exposed household objects and furniture in the ruined city "preserving the memory of love and hatred." Czesław Miłosz, *Zniewolony umysł* [The Captive Mind] (Paris: Instytut Literacki, 1953), 38.

Animate Landscapes I

The Site and the Objects

The site: Czyste, Warsaw, November 2007

Abandoned school room in Pripyat, near Chernobyl

Entrance to the exclusion zone

Czyste landscape

Still from Andrei Tarkovsky's *Stalker*

The site is on the periphery of Warsaw's city center, a peri-urban and desolate landscape of disused rail tracks, low-density commercial lots, nineteenth-century gasometers, and other industrial apparatuses. We discovered this landscape accidentally and explored it through curiosity—a curiosity born of the site's seemingly unique stillness, suggested histories, and ultimately the threat of its perceived fate. In the Edinburgh studio, we decided not to map out the site with a direct representation (such as a site model or plan), as we felt any such representation potentially would be too reductive. We wished to work with the aspects of the site that our curiosity was fixed on, rather than fix or choose aspects of the site from which to draw conclusions (and architecture). In other words, we weren't willing to freeze the site into an idea, but instead wanted to duplicate the site's potential as a question—why were we drawn to it?

The cracked asphalt and derelict train carriages, the decaying buildings of a style that predated Warsaw's near complete annihilation in the mid-twentieth century, and the exposed and redundant rail track that was weighted with so much meaning in the context of this part of the city—these were all reasons we chose the site. Combined, they created a sense of place that was oppositional to the contemporary city's condition—separate from the city while being deeply embedded within it. The threat of

the rapidly expanding city center loomed over the site, a threat of uncertainty and sudden change in condition; a threat present despite the familiarity of the material remnants on the site and the apparent permanence of the landscape's condition.

In many ways, this threat recalled that which lingers in the Zone of Andrei Tarkovsky's 1980 film *Stalker*. The film leads us to believe that the Zone experienced an event that transformed it from an otherwise typical landscape into a place where the rules of the outside world no longer applied. It is this threat of uncertainty in the familiar that we desired to work with and exploit. In order to achieve this, we employed everyday objects, their close and tactile familiarity serving as a staging point for an exploration of uncertainty—the unfamiliar and its potential in design. Our objective, then, was not to create a standpoint to view the site from, but rather to re-create a lack of one.

The exclusion zone around Chernobyl and Pripyat serves as a counterpart to and prophetic realization of Tarkovsky's Zone. In the photographs of abandoned schoolrooms and familiar settings, it is the objects that draw our attention and are the source of our unease as viewers. Their normality and our associations with them encumber us with a sense that the unfamiliar and irreparably altered may infect

The metronome and the plan chest.
Opposite: The metronome scaled up and
placed on the site

and infringe on our own lives. In the case of Chernobyl, it is the lack of human presence that is disturbing—the objects are material entities that survive and outlast us. This unease is at the source of the complexity of the term "resilience." It lies in the witnessing of a newly established normality that has all but replaced a preexisting state. Only the material remnants—objects—connect the two. Through their resiliency, these objects connect us with an unfamiliar, unreachable place, and so have an ambiguous nature—both positive and mournful. In the case of Warsaw, this is further complexified. The annihilation of familiar objects but the continued presence of the contemporary and familiar city develops into a similar sense of unease. Away from Warsaw and the site, searching for objects to work with, we were conscious that the age of the object itself becomes a key factor in linking the studio and site—an antique chair from Edinburgh carries with it a completely different

set of meanings than one found in Warsaw. At first, we worked with the site through a combination of two objects: a worn plan chest and a mechanical metronome. Initially, the objects represented the site figuratively and then, gradually, literally. We started with what they tell us as objects. In the metronome's case, rhythm, time, and tempo—these meanings transcend the object itself, embodied in the signification of the word. The plan chest, as an object in contextual normality, operated as a grounding for this new object, an intermediary between the metronome and the studio. The material of the chest also formed a house for a guide with an intimate bond to the landscape. The guide served to heighten the relationship between the site and the objects, and provided a narrative for the subsequent programming of the site. The plan chest is thus a kind of deception, its familiarity as an object in the context of an architectural studio serving as a departure point for the threat of the unfamiliar—

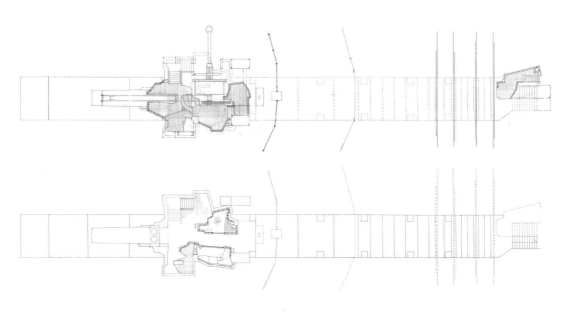

Still from Andrei Tarkovsky's *Stalker*

akin to the lingering shots of natural scenes in the Zone, in which even the trees are infused with menace. The metronome and its placement on the plan chest depict the site as a place outside of time, dominated by the rhythm of the object.

The material conditions of the objects and their relationships to architectural specificities remain unclear to the viewer. The worn and marked surface of the chest alludes to the surface of the ground, the boundary of exploration not yet defined beyond the arbitrary dimensions of the chest. The objects are given an architectural scale, 1:100, and are continually read against each other until the realization that the metronome object now dominates and protects the site, its brass mechanism laid bare and scaled up one hundred times. What we are left with is an embodied resilience. Although the metronome and plan chest have been altered, as things they are largely intact—like the wilderness of the Zone or the toys of Chernobyl. From this, we started to generate a method of working with the site, an attempt to marry the meanings and properties of the landscape as found with the meanings and properties of objects as found. Their initial familiarity as objects provides the tools for a nonexclusive dialogue between the studio and the landscape. One isn't being replaced by the other, rather the objects and the studio embody the landscape we are exploring. Through their reconfiguration, the resilience of the landscape can be revealed and tested.

Ultimately, we created a room of objects within the studio, a meeting point of studio and site, architectural scales and material conditions. The room, like Tarkovsky's room at the center of the Zone, would be a place in which the dreams of the viewer are realized—in which the viewer becomes a participant in a landscape of objects.

Preliminary illustrations embellishing ideas of protection
and preservation through the creation of a localized myth

Inscription device built into table

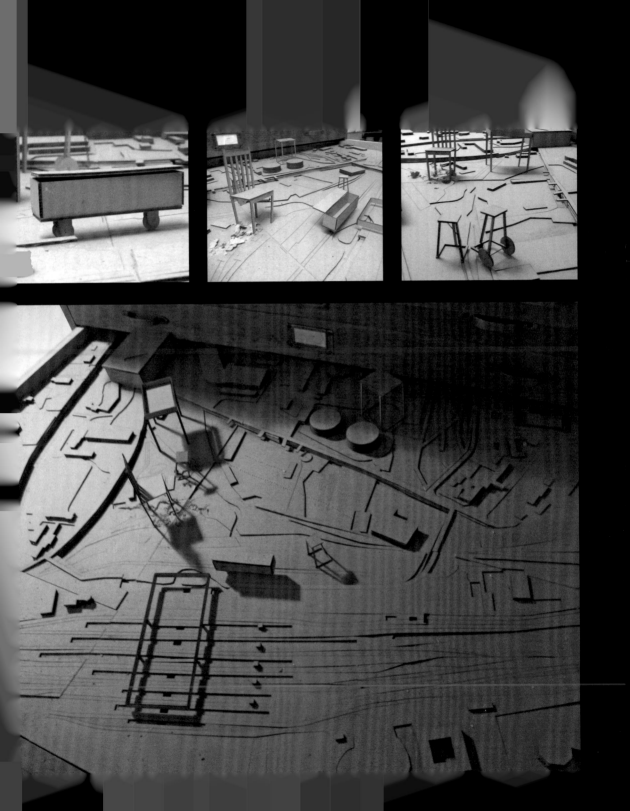

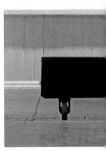

Roll call of objects

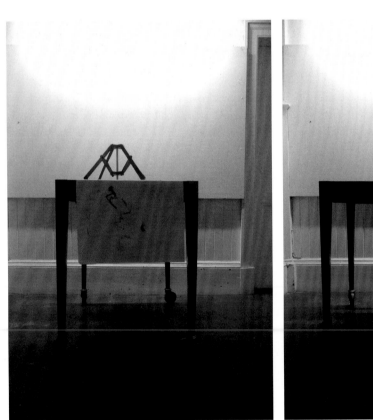

Drafting table with embedded inscription device

The room is the meeting point of studio and site. The utilization of the metronome and the plan chest led us to work with an archive of furniture that aided the development of ideas spatially and materially. Together, the pieces created the recognizable constituent parts of a room, and every object was imbued with an individual agenda and distinct set of meanings.

Each piece of furniture carried its own embodied history of movement, and the project began to remap the imagined animate lives of these now dormant pieces. The metronome had a direct influence over the room and its objects, much in the way that a pianist is guided by the notational language of sheet music; the variant rhythms emanating from the device caused specific reactions in the furniture pieces. Their resulting movements were played out on the site, with each object individually exploring and responding to the terrain of site and studio in different ways. These interactions were executed using a site model built into one of the drawers of the plan chest. Within the drawer, an animation of scenarios was developed that involved each of the furniture pieces (in a scale consistent with the relationship between the plan chest and the metronome). The film focused on the trajectories of each piece, moving to separate speeds or rhythms as generated by the metronome. The slow or fast paces resulted in variant outcomes for the objects in relation to the site and each other.

Collisions, trips, scrapes, and tears on the ground were mapped out by the film, with the furniture hurtling around the site and crashing into each other or with the material remnants on the landscape. In the example of the chair, its movements were mapped along a route toward a junction in the existing railway tracks. Here, in a manner reminiscent of Buster Keaton films, the chair split into two parts, with each half reassigned a rhythm from the metronome's scale. One half of the chair was slower and so moved in a controlled way to its final destination, notionally lodged between two train sheds. The other half was assigned a faster rhythm and so moved chaotically toward a trip over an old factory wall. As with the chair, each piece of furniture had a rhythm assigned and the combined trajectories were played out in varying ways, which ultimately led to a new set of hierarchies between the objects.

The objects:

I	Plan Chest	-
II	Chair Half One	*Larghetto*
III	Chair Half Two	*Adagio*
IV	Toy Box	*Andante*
V	Pedestal	*Largo*
VI	Drafting Table	*Presto*
VII	Pedestal's Brother	*Allegro*
VIII	School Table	-
IX	Bed	-

Furniture trajectories, diagrammatic stages
Opposite: Details of the final stage

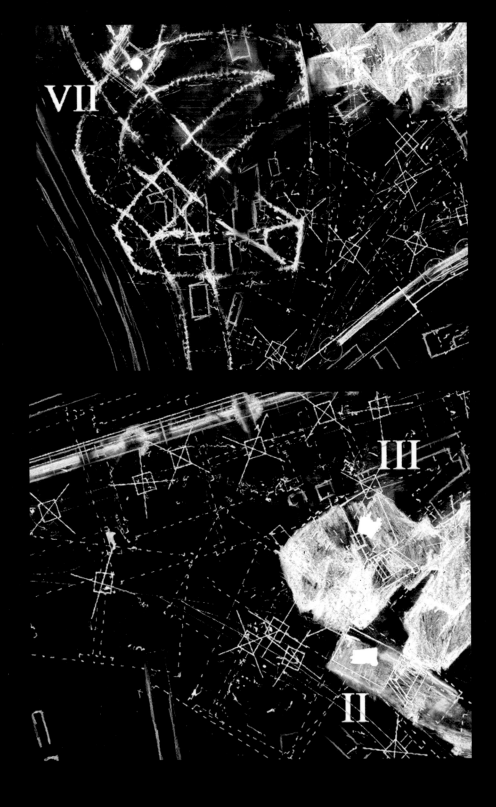

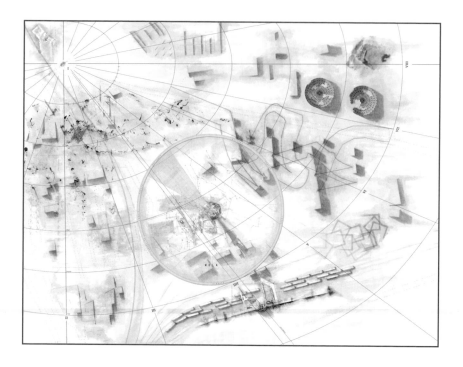

Plan drawing and installation photographs depicting the pieces as arranged in their final resting places after journeying across the site; Opposite: Detail of the inverted observatory chart of movements

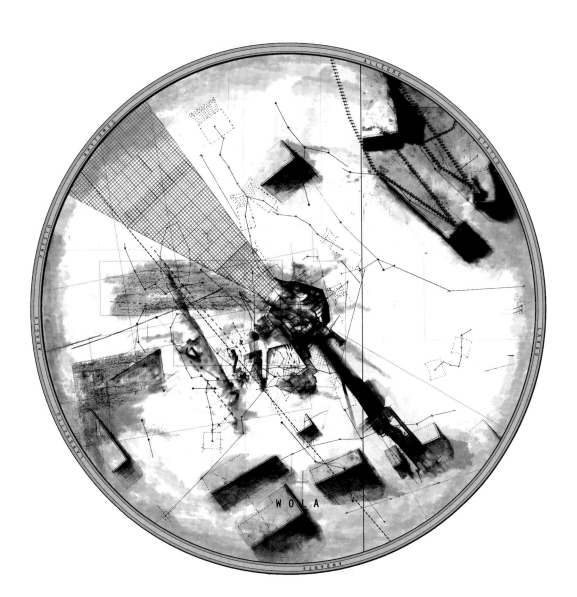

I

VI

VIII

V

III

II

IV

VII

IX

Montaged section through the objects

Inverted observatory model and section

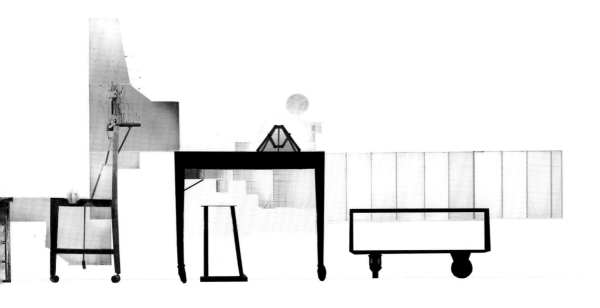

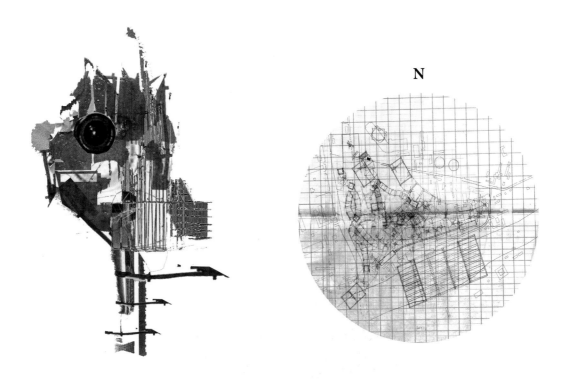

N

Detail of observatory mask and its diagrammatic view of the site

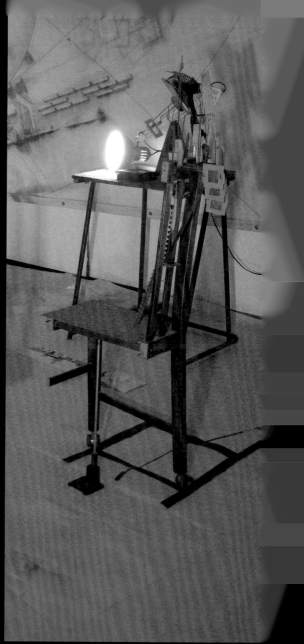

The inverted observatory was developed after the metronome and was conceived as a reactive tool that would keep its gaze fixed firmly on the ground and other objects on the site. The observatory is perched on top of a chair half and, like the metronome, is built at a scale of 1:100 on the 1:1 furniture object. Through the chair's new prosthetic the scales are further blurred—the height of the observatory tower is dictated by the height of the chair's back; here, the furniture directly informs the design of the architectural form. The relational quality of the model is augmented through the integration of a small telescope, which offers the viewer a gaze similar to that in a 1:1 version of the observatory. The chair's role as an observation point, as well as a point of control within a room, is transferred directly to the logic of the site in this development and future objects would react to its constant supervision. Opposite: Detail of toy box and an overview of the

Animate Landscapes III
Antichronometric Calendar

This chapter is to be read as a calendar that uses two voices to describe the site and our process as they developed. One voice is that of the author describing the design process, the other is the voice of the caretaker (our own character, a solitary figure who resides on the site throughout the full duration of the calendar).

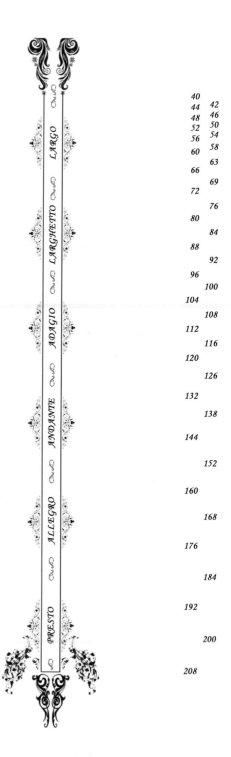

THE PROCEDURE

Author: The antichronometric calendar abides by the tempo of the metronome rather than time as we know it.

The metronome, having dictated the hierarchies present between objects held within the room, now determined the pace of the processes carried out on the site that worked in combination toward a film festival. The festival responded to the means of the site, and the objects were manipulated and interrogated at this stage of the process. Film, photography, and animation were used to critically examine the hierarchies and relationships between objects and site, and from this a program for the site emerged—a national institute of experimental film and an on-site film festival.

The site was activated once the metronome started ticking at the slowest tempo of *largo*. In this phase, the site awakened and the early stages of the filmmaking process began. The fastest tempo, *presto*, harnessed the frenzied time of the festival when production neared completion and films were shown to the public. The festival continued until the metronome ran out of energy and was still again.

LARGO

40

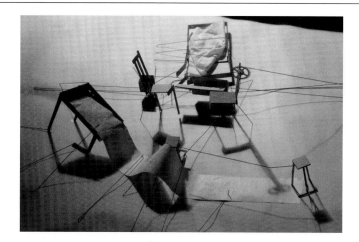

Furniture objects
tethered to the city
beneath

42

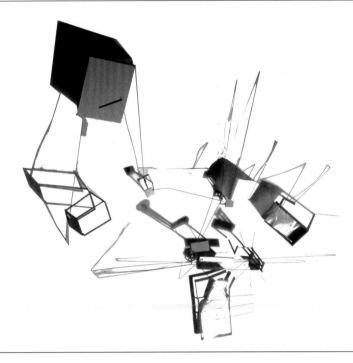

Image blurring the
shadows of objects
with the tethers
that hold them

44

Author: An image (above) was created that concentrated and distilled the animate qualities of the furniture, tethering them to the site and merging the two formerly distinct elements. The manipulated photograph captured the objects in a single image from a potentially animate and timeless sequence of events. The blurring of shadows and physical elements of the model resulted in a frozen moment that served as a territorial master plan for the site. The objects then became the subjects, as they were programmatically defined to form the experimental film institute.

46

The OBJECTS		The SUBJECTS	
I	Plan Chest	I	Metronome
II	Chair Half One	II	Inverted Observatory
III	Chair Half Two	III	Editing Facility
IV	Toy Box	IV	Prop Workshops
V	Pedestal	V	Mirrored Auditoriums
VI	Drafting Table	VI	Soundstage
VII	Pedestal's Brother	VII	Ticket Office
VIII	School Table	VIII	Cinematheque
IX	Bed	IX	Suspended Hotel

48

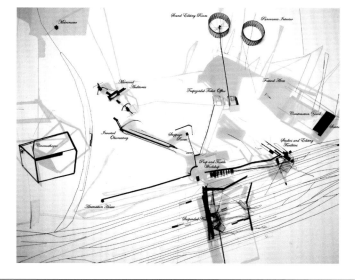

Site model with
image overlay
and programmatic
strategy depicted

50

Author: The intrusions consisted of a series of disparate
structures, each related to a specificity of the filmmaking
process and largely inhabiting the periphery of the existing
landscape. The structures were tied together as if in tension
by gantries and similar walkways that elevated the user from
(and restricted access to) the ground. Through individual
and/or collaborative use of the site, films (along with the
extraneous accretions of the process, e.g., sets, props, excess
film) accumulated and could be presented. This process had a
direct relationship to the tempo of the film studio landscape
as dictated by the metronome. At slower paces, the landscape
appeared serene, with people busy in isolation; as the tempo
rose, the number of people at work on the site, along with the
amount of collaboration and larger-scale production, also
increased. This culminated in the frenzied time of the festival
in which work would be presented in a multiplicity of forms.

52

Caretaker: *I am jolted awake by the slow rhythm of the
metronome as each tick sends a small vibration through my steel
bed frame. Cursing, I open my slot window and see the long
steel arm of the metronome swaying lazily on the horizon. This
is my prompt to prepare the site for the festival. Grudgingly, I
begin my check of the perimeter. I walk 67 paces along the steel
gantry until I come to a junction at which I take a left. Another
417 paces along this intersecting path, I arrive at the trapezoidal
ticket office. I proceed to unlock the door using two keys on a
heavily populated key ring.*

54

Observatory and
auditoriums with
embedded walkway

56

Caretaker: *I pull the heavy lever in the ticket office that sets the cranks of the structure in motion. I watch as the giant metal arms of the trapezoid open up inch by inch, slowly scraping along the ground, pushing up dirt and weeds as they crawl upward. The screech of the straining mechanism is unbearable, and I hurry away.*

58

Gantries connect
the distributed
objects over a
scarred landscape

60

Caretaker: *I leave the ticket office and begin my long journey to the inverted observatory. On the way, I see a stranger on the gantry. Nervous, I nod and shift to let her pass. It has been a long time since anyone used the animation studios she heads toward, and the thought of others makes me uncomfortable.*

63

XI

Garden of dead
reckoning

LARGHETTO

72

Caretaker: *Before I walk the long embedded passage to the base of the inverted observatory, I pause to rest in the garden of dead reckoning. It is a peaceful space, a walled and tiled courtyard in which trapped, half-formed objects merge with pools of dark water. Even the ticking of the metronome is dampened here, though frequent vibrations shudder ripples gently through the water. Looking down at the pools, I can read a map of the site. Or is it a map of its past? The shadow of the observatory looms over me. It is precisely 92 meters tall. There are 396 steps. I begin to climb.*

76

VI

Sequence of
transformations from
furniture objects to
auditoriums

80

Author: The editing facility utilized a long steel needle that lightly touched the tracks of the railway line. The vibrations from the oncoming train caused a disturbance to be channeled into the imaging processing unit. There, the chemicals were splashed around by the vibrations and the artists' images became transformed by the movements of the site.

84

III

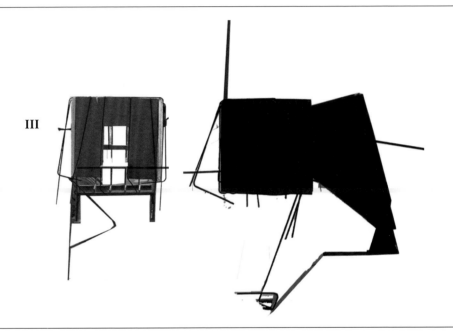

Detail of the editing facility image processing unit

88

Caretaker: *I find myself standing on a wall that rises out of the surface of the ground. I walk on top of it until I come to a series of small rooms. The rooms burst from the terrain, each tethered back into the landscape with long steel cables that I must duck under to progress. Through a window I can see the silhouette of a figure hunched over a faintly glowing screen. I go down into the darkrooms to make sure the processing trays are full.*

96

Stefan Themerson's sketch of his trick table

Author: The editing facility derived from a study into five short experimental films made in Warsaw during the mid-1930s by Stefan and Franciszka Themerson. The experimental techniques of their films were concerned with moving lights and shadows on objects. They evolved out of the Themersons' use of the photogram from 1928 to 1935. Most of the images were made on an improvised trick table. Stefan placed various objects on a piece of translucent paper over a sheet of glass. The lights were above and could be manipulated. He photographed the images from below (frame by frame).

ADAGIO

100

III

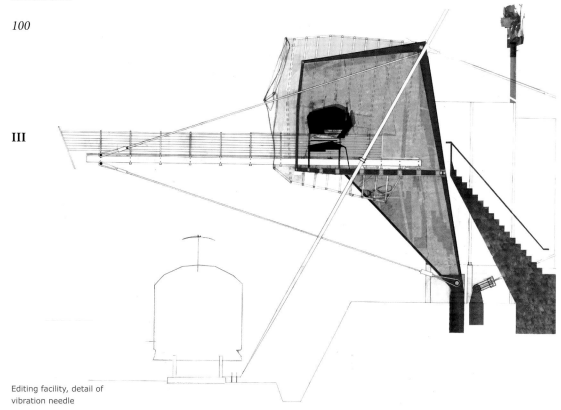

Editing facility, detail of
vibration needle

104

Caretaker: *I must wait for a train to pass in order to test if the equipment in the facility is calibrated and working correctly. I have been waiting in the darkness for thirty-eight minutes. After the train passes I look around, half-blinded, to see my profile captured in a brilliant black on the photo-sensitive paper wall.*

108

Editing facility, early model

112

Caretaker: *Having checked the editing facility's equipment, I head toward the props and textiles workshop. I walk under the giant hammers above the entrance. Their pace is quickening, their rhythm dictating the pace of the activity within. Their incessant pounding stays with me long after I leave.*

120

Author: The bed frame appeared to splinter at its corner as tethers attempted to keep it from sliding along the railway tracks.

126

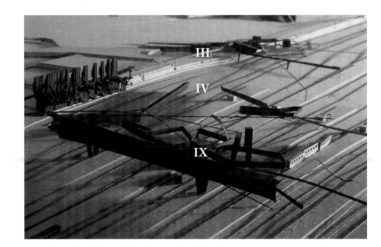

132

1:500 model detail showing the editing facility, prop workshop, and festival hotel

ANDANTE

138

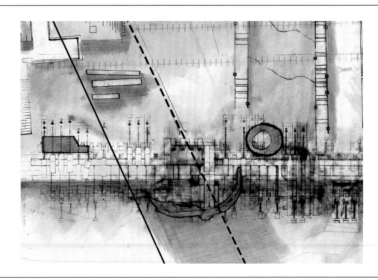

IV

Prop and textile workshop

144

Caretaker: *Having completed my rounds I make my way to the suspended hotel for the night. My room is made of timber; it is warm and dry as rain runs down the rusting steel shell around it.*

ALLEGRO

152

160

IX

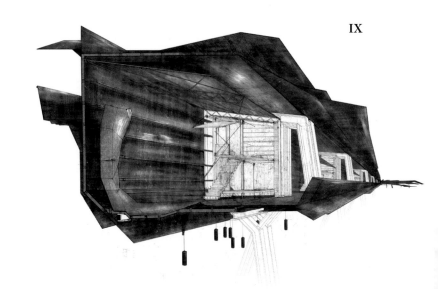

Festival hotel, room detail

168

Author: The hotel was a steel shell, open to the elements. In this carapace, intimate manipulable timber shelters were nestled. These opened up, revealing pristine and opulent interiors for use of the esteemed festival guests. The hotel was held above Zachodnia train station, a link to the city.

184

Caretaker: *The artists are arriving at a greater frequency. I can tell from the echo of footsteps on the gantries. I go to the suspended hotel bar and serve myself a large vodka and apple juice. I notice my hands are trembling. More and more people are arriving at the train platforms just below my feet. A small buggy wheels into the center of the structure on a track. It attaches a hydraulic tail into the wall and inflates the room; suddenly, tables, chairs, and a chandelier are pushed out from the steel structure. I quickly finish my drink and leave.*

176

Author: The hotel was only used in the festival (at presto). This was the case for several of the object/subjects. For the remainder of the time, they operated as signals to the city of the status of the site: antichronometric devices for reading the landscape.

192

Caretaker: *The chaotic vibrations on the site are enough to tell me that it is festival time again. In the distance, the metronome is a blur of movement. I take my key, study it for a long moment, then open the gates.*

PRESTO

200

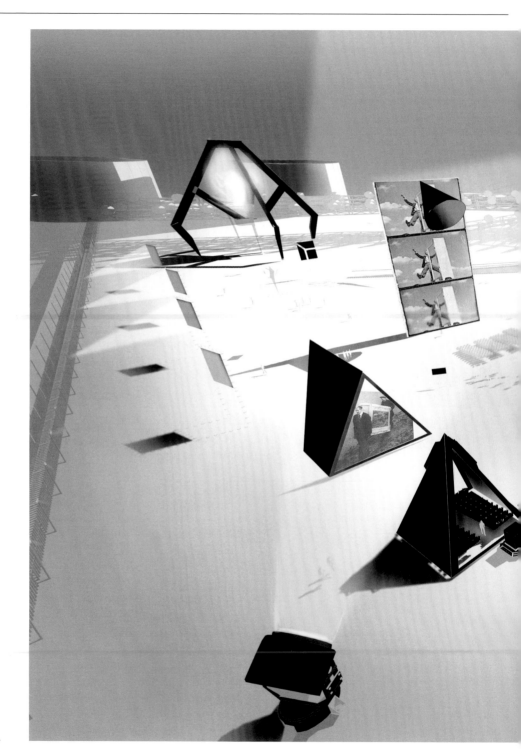

208

The festival begins.

Animate Landscapes IV
The Room

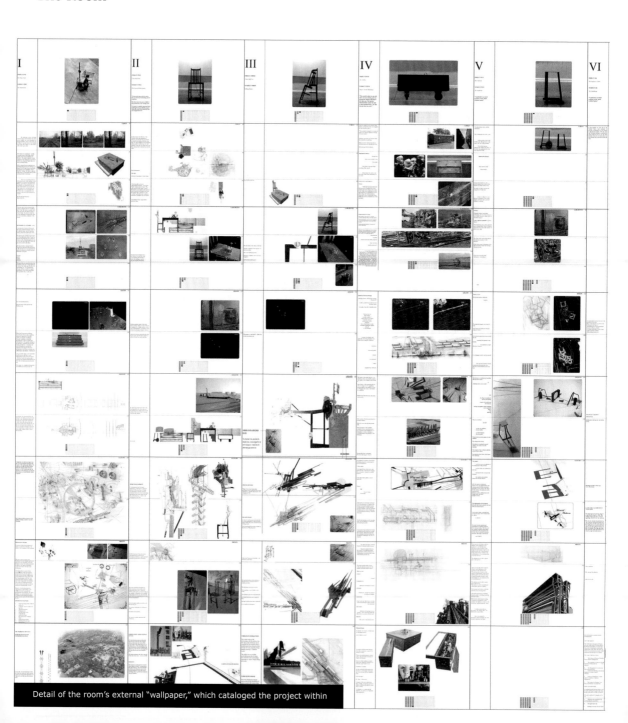

Detail of the room's external "wallpaper," which cataloged the project within

…enter…

Above the entrance is a broken clock on which the numerals have melted. As I enter the room, I am plunged into darkness. Only the surface glimmer of an expansive metal structure held just above waist height is visible. At first, it seems difficult to move beyond this structure; it spreads across the enclosure and is tethered like a steel web. Objects are held within it. A small coin box is attached to the entrance; I put a coin in and hear the release of the barrier. On closer inspection, the barrier is a miniature walkway, a delicate pathway suspended above nothingness. Gently, I lift the barrier and move into the center of the room. To my left, a film plays on a small screen. It shows a landscape of objects moving in time to the rhythm of a metronome. The incessant ticking is the only sound in the room. I look down to see a train passing under my feet. Pulses emanate across the floor, originating from the far side of the room. The half-light shows this space to be free of the steel tethers, and I head toward it. I pass a masked device, expressionlessly watching me. Another object seems to emerge from the steel itself, trapped against the walls. There are smaller rooms within, and I clamber through them. I traverse a long walkway, attempting not to look down. I see the towering observatory, its lens curiously directed toward the ground. I climb it; the never-ending flight of stairs puts an intolerable strain on my calves. I gaze through its eye and see the metronome. I walk toward the back of the room where the device is positioned, wind it up, and set it at a new rhythm, faster now. I walk away at a similar pace; the rhythm emanates far beyond the enclosure as I leave.

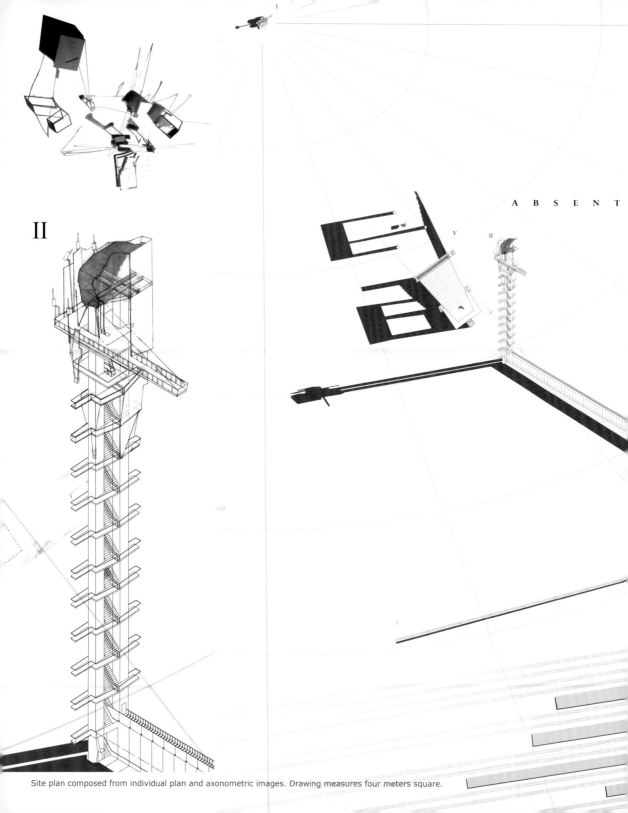

I

II

A B S E N T

V

II

VIII

Site plan composed from individual plan and axonometric images. Drawing measures four meters square.

1:10 ROOM PLAN

1:1000 SITE PLAN

WINDOW

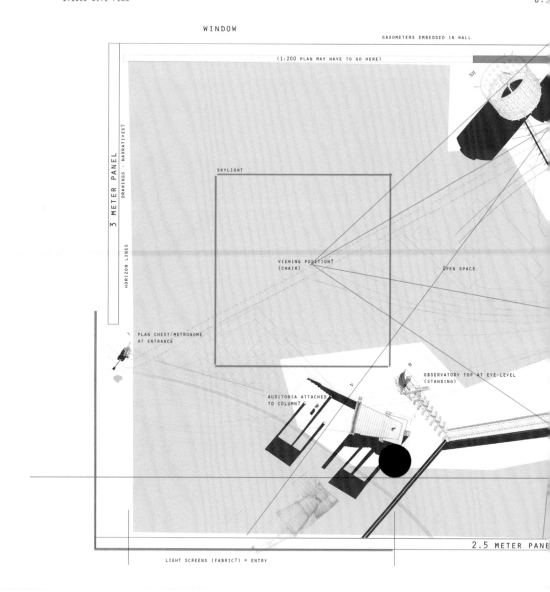

GASOMETERS EMBEDDED IN WALL

(1:200 PLAN MAY HAVE TO GO HERE)

3 METER PANEL

DRAWINGS - NARRATIVES?

HORIZON LINES

SKYLIGHT

VIEWING POSITION?
(CHAIR)

OPEN SPACE

PLAN CHEST/METRONOME
AT ENTRANCE

OBSERVATORY TOP AT EYE-LEVEL
(STANDING)

AUDITORIA ATTACHED
TO COLUMN?

2.5 METER PANE

LIGHT SCREENS (FABRIC?) + ENTRY

Working drawing of the room incorporating site plan at 1:100

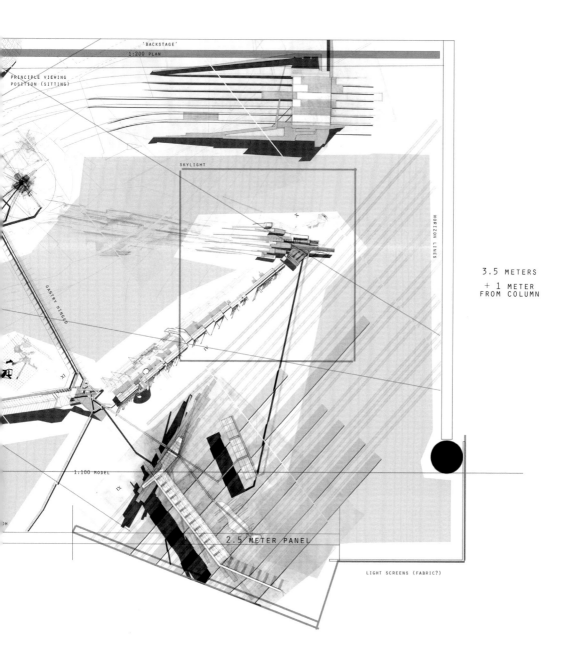

'BACKSTAGE'
1:200 PLAN

PRINCIPLE VIEWING
POSITION (SITTING)

SKYLIGHT

HORIZON LINES

GANTRY HINGED

1:100 MODEL

3.5 METERS
+ 1 METER
FROM COLUMN

2.5 METER PANEL

LIGHT SCREENS (FABRIC?)

Construction sequence of the room
Opposite: Details of the construction

Suspended hotel, walkway gate
Opposite: Trapezoidal ticket office, prop and textile workshops

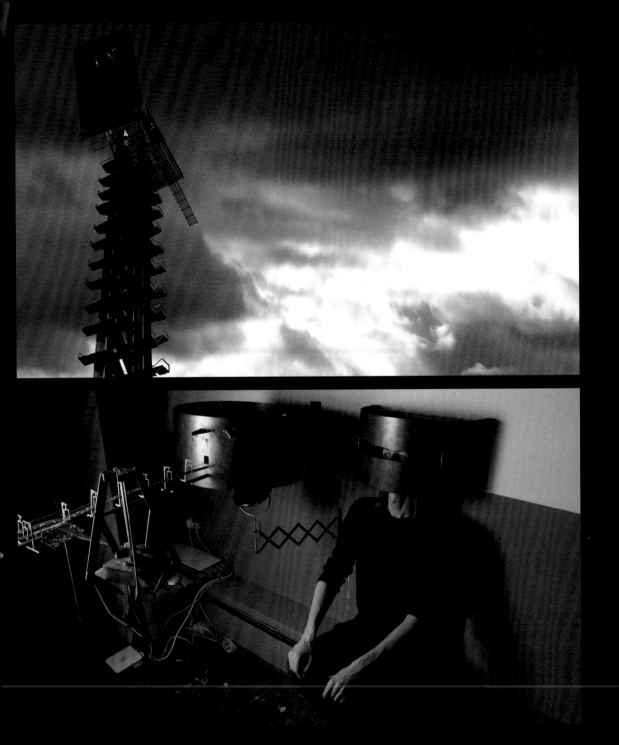

Inverted observatory, horizon-line panoramic viewing device
Opposite: Metronome, platforms and ladders behind the mask of the observatory, concealed hotel rooms

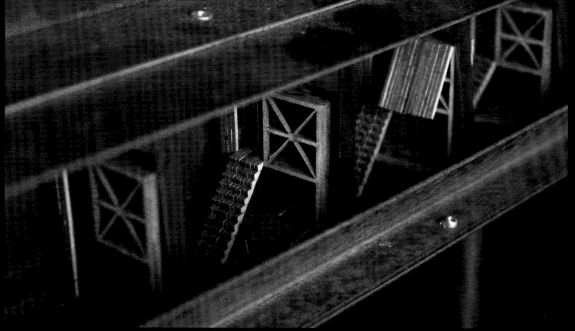

Echo chamber sound recording room held in a derelict gasometer, trapezoidal ticket office, overview of the room
Opposite: Observatory above screen one of the mirrored auditoriums

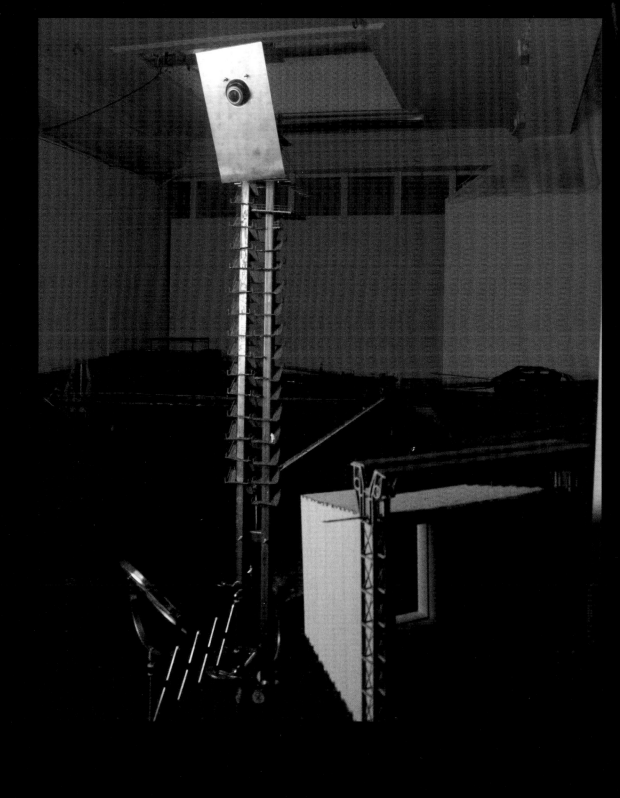

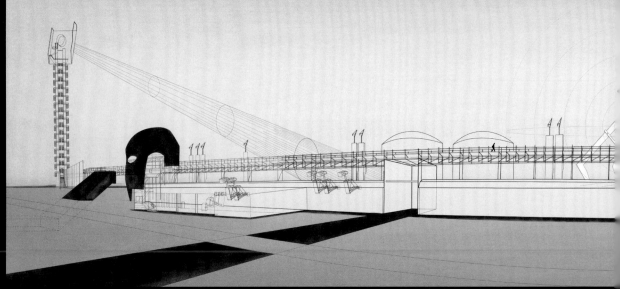

Garden of dead reckoning, panoramic drawing of the site as seen from a passing train
Opposite: Editing facility

Designing Around Remnants

Andrew Benjamin

If there is a set of questions that should exercise a determining hold on urban design, then it is staged by the ineliminability of the remnant. The remnant is the mark that continues to endure. These marks can be as much material as they are immaterial, combining the physical characteristics of place and questions of memory. Equally, however, the persistence of the remnant has another quality, understood as the focus of a specific desire. This desire, which is as central to metaphysics as it is to architecture, is for destruction (the elimination of the remnant as a material presence) in order to overcome memory and enforce a sense of forgetting. Allowing remnants to remain, therefore, is to resist equating destruction with either elimination or forgetting.

The remnant enables the co-presence of destruction and creation. Creation occurs by recognizing or holding onto the remnant. This is a form of destruction precisely because any intervention in a site is a destructive act. In addition, creative acts that are not predetermined open up a range of possibilities that require reworking and repositioning the remnant. The remnant is retained by allowing it to prompt design, giving it a determining role either in the design process or within the actual project. Maintaining remnants, therefore, is to incorporate in the design the remnant's link to the materiality of place and the immateriality of memory.

The project undertaken here, Animate Landscapes, involves a doubled sense of the remnant. The doubling becomes the inscription of two histories: one that pertains to the studio and one to Warsaw (the project's ostensible site). Within both settings, found objects, images, vestiges of an inchoate and contextual past begin to form another space, one of creation and invention.

Resilience is a quality that can be attributed to remnants. Within that context, the project deploys its own devices: the metronome, chairs, images, etc. These elements begin to form a setting that activates the model. This is a model that does more than recall the site. More is in place. The most striking words that occur in the project's description are the following: "To walk around the model is to walk around the site." What would it mean if this were true? As a beginning, it would imply that the language of representation, both conceptual and practical, has been displaced. In its stead, there are projects of mapping and drawing in which two sites were constructed: studio and building site. Both of these theaters of concerns represent a staging of architectural events whose presence eschew that separation, in which the reality of one is refracted through the abstract quality of the other. Forever standing in the way of such a neat disjunction would be the remnants, whose presence is yet another form of resilience.

Andrew Benjamin is Professor of Critical Theory at Monash University.

Acknowledgments

"What if?" This question, posed repeatedly by Mark Dorrian throughout the design process detailed in this pamphlet, embodies the significance of his pedagogy and its value for our relationship—equals in a reciprocal process. The question frames potentialities rather than specifying a response. It invites an intellectual discovery. It demands rigor without setting limits. For giving space to our ideas and inspiring us to explore their resiliency, Mark, we are truly grateful. We would like to thank Ella Chmielewska for introducing us to Warsaw and its histories, surfaces, and spaces. We are grateful to Andrew Benjamin for providing closure for the work in this pamphlet. We thank Katy Bentall for creating and holding the studio space on Smolna Street, which would influence us more than we could know. We are indebted to Keith Milne, whose craft and photography are featured in these pages.

Many thanks to our friends and families for their support and enthusiasm. And finally, our gratitude goes to Pamphlet Architecture, Princeton Architectural Press, and our editor, Megan Carey, for their support in the production of this pamphlet.

About the Authors

James A. Craig and Matt Ozga-Lawn are the principals of Stasus, a UK-based studio developed as a continuing platform for architectural design and discourse. Their projects have been exhibited at the Royal Scottish Academy in Edinburgh in 2008, the Zacheta Gallery of Modern Art in Warsaw in 2008, Generator Projects in Dundee in 2010, and most recently at the Summer Exhibition 2011 at the Royal Academy of Arts in London.

Craig is an independent architect and artist living and working in London. He graduated from the University of Edinburgh and has been project architect for a number of practices in the UK. He has reviewed at the Bartlett School of Architecture and the University of Westminster.

Ozga-Lawn is a PhD candidate at Newcastle University enrolled in the newly established PhD by Creative Practice, and his research continues the methodology described in this pamphlet. He has taught and reviewed at the University of Edinburgh and is an undergraduate studio tutor at Newcastle University.

www.stasus.com

Image Credits: All images courtesy of the authors unless otherwise noted. 4: Tereska, courtesy of the Bodleian Library, Oxford; 8: Aerial photograph, courtesy of Cartographic Section, National Archives; 10: Warsaw Surface, courtesy of Paul Keskeys; 11: Still from Street of Crocodiles, courtesy of the Brothers Quay; 12: Katy Bentall's studio, courtesy of Mark Dorrian; 15: Alphonse Bertillon exhibition, courtesy of the National Gallery of Canada; 16–17: Animate Objects installation photograph, courtesy of Keith Miln; 22: Chair and Mask, courtesy of Simon Johnson; 28: Classrooms in Kindergarten #7, "Golden Key," Pripyat, courtesy of Robert Polidori; 29: Entrance to the Zone of Alienation around Chernobyl, courtesy of Slawojar; 29: Still from Stalker, courtesy of The Robert Grant Archive, London; 32: Still from Stalker, courtesy of FSUE Mosfilm Cinema Concern, Moscow; 78–79: Objects III and IX photographs, courtesy of Keith Milne

III: Editing facility model

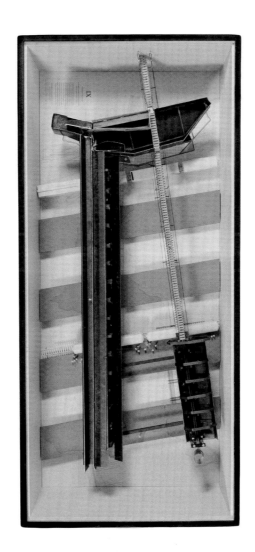

IX: Suspended hotel model

Pamphlet Architecture

Pamphlet Architecture was initiated in 1977 as an independent vehicle to criticize, question, and exchange views. Each issue is assembled by an individual author/architect. For information, Pamphlet proposals, or contributions, please write to: Pamphlet Architecture, c/o Princeton Architectural Press, 37 East 7th Street, New York, NY 10003, or go to www.pamphletarchitecture.org.

Pamphlets published:

1.	Bridges	S. Holl	1977*
2.	10 California Houses	M. Mack	1978*
3.	Villa Prima Facie	L. Lerup	1978*
4.	Stairwells	L. Dimitriu	1979*
5.	Alphabetical City	S. Holl	1980
6.	Einstein Tomb	L. Woods	1980*
7.	Bridge of Houses	S. Holl	1981*
8.	Planetary Architecture	Z. Hadid	1981*
9.	Rural and Urban House Types	S. Holl	1981*
10.	Metafisica della Architettura	A. Sartoris	1984*
11.	Hybrid Buildings	J. Fenton	1985
12.	Building; Machines	R. McCarter	1987
13.	Edge of a City	S. Holl	1991
14.	Mosquitoes	K. Kaplan, T. Krueger	1993
15.	War and Architecture	L. Woods	1993
16.	Architecture as a Translation of Music	E. Martin	1994
17.	Small Buildings	M. Caldwell	1996
19.	Reading Drawing Building	M. Silver	1996
20.	Seven Partly Underground Rooms	M. A. Ray	1997
21.	Situation Normal...	Lewis.Tsurumaki.Lewis	1998
22.	Other Plans	Michael Sorkin Studio	2001
23.	Move	J. S. Dickson	2002
24.	Some Among Them Are Killers	D. Ross	2003
25.	Gravity	J. Cathcart et al.	2003
26.	13 Projects for the Sheridan Expressway	J. Solomon	2004
27.	Tooling	Aranda/Lasch	2006
28.	Augmented Landscapes	Smout Allen	2007
29.	Ambiguous Spaces	Naja & deOstos	2008
30.	Coupling	InfraNet Lab/Lateral Office	2011
31.	New Haiti Villages	S. Holl	2011

*out of print, available only in the collection *Pamphlet Architecture 1–10*.